FARM ANIMALS

DONKEYS

by Michelle Hasselius

Consultant: Dr Mark Z. Johnson
Department of Animal Science
Oklahoma State University, USA

raintree

a Capstone company — publishers for children

Raintree is an imprint of Capstone Global Library Limited, a company incorporated in England and Wales having its registered office at 264 Banbury Road, Oxford, OX2 7DY – Registered company number: 6695582

www.raintree.co.uk
myorders@raintree.co.uk

Text © Capstone Global Library Limited 2017
The moral rights of the proprietor have been asserted.

Printed and bound in China.

Editorial credits
Michelle Hasselius, editor; Kayla Rossow, designer; Pam Mitsakos, media researcher;
Katy LaVigne, production specialist

ISBN 978 1 4747 2241 4
20 19 18 17 16
10 9 8 7 6 5 4 3 2 1

British Library Cataloguing in Publication Data
A full catalogue record for this book is available from the British Library.

Acknowledgements
Shutterstock: Andrei Ovasko, 6–7, ChiccoDodiFC, 19, Daniel Wilson, 13, Dennis W. Donohue, 9, DragoNika, cover, Eky Studio, (back cover background), Elena Larina, 16–17, Elenamiv, 22 (background), Elisa Locci, 10–11, Germano Poli, 15, Kookkai_nak, 1 (background), Menna, 1; Thinkstock: jtyler, 5, Purestock, 20–21

The author would like to thank Dr Mark Z. Johnson for his invaluable help in the preparation of this book.

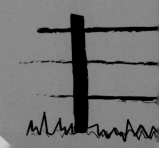

Contents

Meet the donkeys

Hee-haw! The donkeys bray loudly on the farm. The sound can be heard from far away. Donkeys bray to communicate with each other.

Donkeys have shaggy coats.

Many donkeys are grey.

But they can also be black,

brown, red-brown or white.

Some are even spotted.

There are three types of donkey. Miniatures are less than 0.9 metres (3 feet) tall. Standards are 0.9 to 1.4 metres tall. Mammoths are more than 1.4 metres (4.6 feet) tall.

miniature donkey

There are more than 44 million donkeys in the world. Many live on farms. Donkeys weigh up to 258 kilograms (570 pounds). They can live for 25 years or more.

Adults and babies

Donkeys grow up on the farm.

Male donkeys are called jacks.

Females are called jennies.

Foals are baby donkeys. They

stand and walk soon after birth.

jenny

foal

On the farm

Donkeys spend their time in fenced pastures. They eat grass and hay. Donkeys also need a stable or barn. It protects donkeys from rain, wind and snow.

Donkeys are strong. They can carry heavy loads on their backs. Donkeys can also pull carts. Long ago farmers used donkeys to plough fields.

A donkey's role

Today farmers use donkeys to protect sheep, cattle and goats. Donkeys do not like foxes and dogs. Donkeys bray and chase them away from the herds.

Donkeys can be kept as pets.

Farmers also use donkeys

to calm nervous horses.

The donkey stays with the

horse in the stable and pasture.

Glossary

bray make a loud, harsh noise

coat animal's fur or wool

communicate share information, thoughts or feelings

herd large group of animals that lives or moves together

nervous scared or timid

pasture land where farm animals eat grass and exercise

plough turn over soil before seeds are planted

stable building or part of a building where farm animals are kept; animals such as donkeys, horses and cattle use stables

Read more

Animals on the Farm (Animals I Can See), Sian Smith (Raintree, 2015)

A Nature Walk on the Farm (Nature Walks), Louise and Richard Spilsbury (Heinemann Library, 2015)

Donkeys (Animals), Darice Bailer (Marshall Cavendish Benchmark, 2012)

Websites

www.abc.net.au/creaturefeatures/facts/donkeys.htm
Learn interesting facts about and the history of donkeys.

ypte.org.uk/factsheets/donkeys/the-donkey#section
Read about domestic and wild donkeys, as well as how donkeys compare to horses.